The Planets

Your Mission to Jupiter

by Nadia Higgins
illustrated by Scott Burroughs

Content Consultant
Diane M. Bollen, Research Scientist,
Cornell University

magic
wagon

visit us at www.abdopublishing.com

Published by Magic Wagon, a division of the ABDO Group, 8000 West 78th
Street, Edina, Minnesota, 55439. Copyright © 2012 by Abdo Consulting
Group, Inc. International copyrights reserved in all countries. All rights
reserved. No part of this book may be reproduced in any form without
written permission from the publisher.

Looking Glass Library™ is a trademark and logo of Magic Wagon.

Printed in the United States of America, North Mankato, Minnesota.
052011
092011
 THIS BOOK CONTAINS AT LEAST 10% RECYCLED MATERIALS.

Text by Nadia Higgins
Illustrations by Scott Burroughs
Edited by Holly Saari
Design and production by Becky Daum

Library of Congress Cataloging-in-Publication Data
Higgins, Nadia.
  Your mission to Jupiter / by Nadia Higgins ; illustrated by Scott Burroughs.
     p. cm. — (The planets)
  Includes index.
  ISBN 978-1-61641-678-2
  1. Jupiter (Planet)—Juvenile literature. I. Burroughs, Scott, ill. II. Title.
  QB661.H54 2012
  523.45—dc22
                          2011005919

Table of Contents

Imagine You Could Go

You couldn't really go to Jupiter. The atmosphere is so heavy it would crush you flat. Or powerful winds would tear you to pieces. Or heat or cold would boil or freeze you.

Nobody has ever traveled to Jupiter. But imagine if you could . . .

You can easily see Jupiter without a telescope. It looks slightly orange in the night sky.

Solar System

A map of the solar system will help you find your way. All eight planets orbit the sun. Jupiter is the fifth planet from the sun.

Jupiter's Size

Jupiter is by far the largest and heaviest planet. Imagine you could squash all the other planets into one. That new planet would only be half as heavy as Jupiter!

If Jupiter were a giant bag, you could stuff more than 1,400 Earths inside it.

Years and Days

A year on Earth is 365 days. That's how long it takes Earth to orbit the sun. But a year on Jupiter is 4,332 days. It takes the giant planet almost 12 Earth years to orbit the sun once.

Besides orbiting, the planets also spin like tops. One spin equals one day. On Earth, a day is 24 hours. A day on Jupiter is less than 10 hours. It is the fastest-spinning planet.

5

Jupiter's Appearance

As you get close to Jupiter, you gasp a little. It's so beautiful. You gaze at its swirling stripes of red, brown, orange, and white.

The stripes are made from clouds of gases. Strong winds blow them around the planet. The stripes move at different levels in the sky. That's why they don't get mixed together.

Squinting, you see ovals inside the stripes. Those are storms. They come and go every few days.

One oval is much bigger than the others. It is a reddish color. That is why it's called the Great Red Spot. This giant storm is wider than Earth and Mars combined! It has been raging for at least 300 years.

Temperature and Gravity

In Jupiter's highest clouds, it's colder than any place on Earth. But as you fly lower and lower, the temperature gets hotter and hotter. The atmosphere gets thicker and thicker.

By now, your arms and legs feel very heavy. Jupiter's powerful gravity makes your jet pack feel like heavy rocks.

Gravity is a powerful force in the universe. Gravity on Earth is what pulls things to the ground. Jupiter's gravity is two-and-a-half times as strong as Earth's gravity.

Gases

If this were Earth, you'd land on the ground. But Jupiter has no land. Its outer layer is made of gases. The gases are mostly hydrogen and helium. They are the same gases that make up the sun. And they are poisonous.

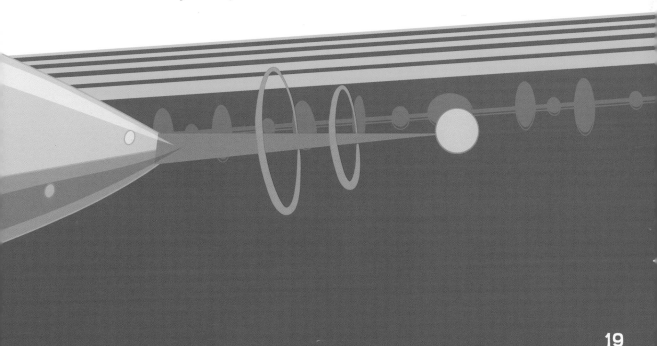

Liquid and Core

Now, the gases are super thick. Eventually, you find yourself splashing in an ocean of liquid hydrogen.

You swim down for thousands of miles. Under the ocean, you find out what Jupiter's core is made of. Scientists believe the planet has a heavy, thick center. Is that true? You write down your important discovery.

At 45,000 degrees Fahrenheit (25,000°C), Jupiter's core is thought to be very hot. It is about 450 times hotter than the steamiest summer day on Earth!

Jupiter's Moons

You're tired by now. But you still want to see Jupiter's famous moons. The planet has more than 60 of them. Jupiter's strong gravity pulls on the moons. That keeps the moons orbiting Jupiter, just as planets orbit the sun.

First, you travel to Io, one of Jupiter's four biggest moons. This yellowish moon is rocky, like Earth. As you fly around it, you see volcanoes erupting. You count how many volcanoes you see and write down the number. Scientists believe it could be as many as 300!

25

On the moon Europa, you perform a very special mission. You drill down through the icy crust. Is liquid water sloshing there? Scientists really want to know. They think the water could be a sign of life.

Scientists believe Europa could have twice as much water as Earth.

On Ganymede, you write your mom a postcard: "Greetings from the solar system's largest moon!" On Callisto, you wish your friends were with you to see the amazing craters.

You had a great time visiting Jupiter. But as you climb back into your rocket, you can't wait to return to planet Earth.

How Do Scientists Know about Jupiter?

Since ancient times, people have watched Jupiter in the night sky. In the early 1600s, the Italian Galileo began using a telescope to study space. Through this important tool, Galileo saw four of Jupiter's biggest moons. They were orbiting the planet. Back then, everyone believed that the sun, stars, and everything else in space orbited Earth. Galileo's discovery showed this was not so.

Scientists continued to look at Jupiter through telescopes. In the 1970s, the National Aeronautics and Space Administration (NASA) started sending spacecraft to Jupiter. These spacecraft flew without astronauts, but they could still collect important data. *Pioneers 10* and *11* helped map the planet. Then in 1979, *Voyagers 1* and *2* took close-up images of Jupiter's moons. Still, these spacecraft only flew by Jupiter.

In 1995, *Galileo* was the first spacecraft to orbit Jupiter. For eight years, it traveled around the planet and its moons. Thanks to the *Galileo* mission, scientists discovered evidence of water on Europa. And, they learned more about Io's volcanoes.

The next NASA mission to Jupiter is set to arrive on the planet in 2016. Scientists hope that the *Juno* spacecraft will go deep inside the planet. They hope to learn much more about what the giant planet is made of.

Jupiter Facts

Position: Fifth planet from sun

Distance from sun: 483 million miles (778 million km)

Diameter (distance through the planet's middle): 88,900 miles (143,000 km)

Length of orbit (year): Almost 12 Earth years

Length of rotation (day): About 10 hours

Gravity: Two-and-a-half times stronger than Earth's gravity

Number of moons: More than 60

Main moons: Io, Europa, Ganymede, and Callisto

Important features: Colored bands of clouds and the Great Red Spot

Words to Know

atmosphere—the layer of gases surrounding a planet.

core—the center of a planet.

crater—a dip in the ground shaped like a large bowl.

gas—a substance that spreads out to fit what it is in, like air in a tire.

gravity—the force that pulls a smaller object toward a larger object.

orbit—to travel around something, usually in an oval path.

solar system—a star and the objects, such as planets, that travel around it.

volcano—a mountain from which hot liquid rock or steam comes out.

Learn More

Books

Allyn, Daisy. *Jupiter: The Largest Planet.* New York: Gareth Stevens, 2011.

Landau, Elaine. *Jupiter.* New York: Children's Press, 2008.

Whiting, Sue. *Ancient Orbiters: A Guide to the Planets.* Washington DC: National Geographic, 2006.

Web Sites

To learn more about Jupiter, visit ABDO Group online at **www.abdopublishing.com**. Web sites about Jupiter are featured on our Book Links page. These links are routinely monitored and updated to provide the most current information available.

Index